Metaphysics and Coffee

Jeremy Paul Amick

PublishAmerica
Baltimore

© 2006 by Jeremy Paul Amick.
All rights reserved. No part of this book may be reproduced, stored in a retrieval system or transmitted in any form or by any means without the prior written permission of the publishers, except by a reviewer who may quote brief passages in a review to be printed in a newspaper, magazine or journal.

First printing

At the specific preference of the author, PublishAmerica allowed this work to remain exactly as the author intended, verbatim, without editorial input.

ISBN: 1-4241-2781-5
PUBLISHED BY PUBLISHAMERICA, LLLP
www.publishamerica.com
Baltimore

Printed in the United States of America

This book is dedicated to the two women in my life who keep me on the straight-and-narrow; my beautiful wife Amillia and my mother Linda. I would also like to dedicate this to the memory of Jim Morrison and Jack Kerouac for your profound influence on my writing. Thank you one and all.

Metaphysics and Coffee

Metaphysics and coffee
Provide a lap dance for my soul
Creating refreshing and eurhythmic scenes
That my mind can't easily depose

The day of reckoning does approach
When I must reconcile my actions with faith
While the impetuous question rattles in my mind,
"Will this occur before it's too late?"

I treat myself with grave ruthlessness
Pushing the envelope to questionable bounds
My oligarchy of dictatorial demons
May bequeath me only shame as a crown

Working Folks

Understandable illumination
Amorphous funding
Take away from those who earn
Forced adjustment to new standards
Indulge the lazy
Crucify the working
Secrets will writhe in the light
When the rock of truth is overturned

Wretched Cluster

Dozens of huddled guilt-stricken hearts
Wretchedly clustered in the bowels of the foreboding church
Several detached minds writhe in tangled anguish
Knowing they've not found true faith in their corporeal search

The life they have been living—less than respectable
The horrible wear on a tormented heart
Is it ever too late to do what is right?
And if not, who is making the calls

To the "Great One" they turn when all hope seems lost
When times are well, Christmas and Easter are enough
To seek his mercy and the warmth of his blessings
While the faithful stay true through sickness and loss

They now pray that his grace and whispered mercy extend
To those who eventually turn face on past transgressions
And welcome them back to the flock of the faithful
With open arms and an eternal home in heaven

Trekking for Love…Don't Look Back

To my understanding and most patient beauty
Just a small token of my stalwart affection
Please accept this with an open heart
And forget any past frustrations

As our future slowly draws nigh
Many good things are yet to come
Let's walk through this life always together
Yet not forget just how far we have come

Searching For The One

Relocation.
Military.
Just three hours north of home.
Though still wandering the vast
Desert of loneliness.
Searching.
One companion.
The one.
Where?
When?
I'm tired of waiting.
Losing my head.
Hopes becoming stagnant
Languid
Oh, but to be so young and sexually uninhibited
Yet static.
Well, they can have it.

The Transition of Seasons

In the warmth of a February spring-pleasant day
I watch the snow as it fades slowly away
With hopes that the cold withered times will be gone
To give way to the spring and her rains so strong

Spring will concede to the summer so blistery
Making the days of winter seem like a distant memory
But the suns blazing rays will also grow old
Making us yearn for the times that we despised as too cold

Then autumn prances in with her colors so fine
Reminding us that Mother Nature is truly divine
Then back to the cold winter days as before
These once welcomed seasons we soon will deplore

Aplomb

Come on,
Come on,
Come with me.
These types of people,
We don't need.

You can fight them,
But they have the guns.
All we know,
Is how to have fun.

Last night in my sleep,
I had a great vision,
People followed,
And we started a religion.

It will only be us few,
Only our kind.
We will be respected,
For our developing minds.

Do you understand,
My great vision?
Hurry up and make,
Your decision.

The sooner the better,
I've always heard.
We will soon soar,
As majestic as birds.

We can sing what we want,
We'll write our own poetry.
You don't have to conform to their rules,
Yourself you can be.

Do you understand,
My great vision?
Are you going,
To make a decision?

What is it you'll miss?
Your parents babying you?
Well someday they'll die,
Then what will you do?

Come with us.
Trust and believe.
And when your parents are gone,
Then you can grieve.

Don't you see,
That you're one of us?
We're all brothers and sisters,
We've learned how to trust.

Overpopulation

Soon we will be rubbing shoulders
Difficult to breathe
Disease, natural disaster, famine or war
Chinese hell.
Procreation.
It might never end.

Future in Full Hindsight

Everything at once goes wrong.
But, then for a few flashing moments,
Everything is great,
Strange affixation with living.
Death I do recall.
Keep trying.
Full speed ahead to nowhere and nothing.

Let It Rest

Death.
Such a dreary word
Many a time
That thought has occurred
It sneaks upon us slowly
Although we know it's there
It adds to our dreams
The element of fear
I once heard someone say
All good things must end
To those who don't believe me
I don't mean to offend
I just tell it how I see it
The honest way is the best
Now that I've expressed my thoughts
I'll lay this subject to rest

Stones

The cold stones,
Lock me in.
I want to crawl,
Back in my den.
I want to hide,
Don't make me learn.
Send me to Hell,
I'd rather burn.
Now I am free,
With nothing planned.
Can I make it?
Yes, I can.

Manipulation

Give me a world
Make it all mine
I will toy with it
All of the time
Do what I want
I am my boss
To me
There is no loss
Develop the land
Make automobiles
How does this progress
Make you feel
Now it's all done for
It's all used up
It makes me feel
….Very corrupt

Baseless Worries

I am not worried
About the end of my life
Everyone will drop
From this consuming strife

Each religion
Possesses a view
Buddhists, Pagans
Christians and Jews

The pain will be over
No more worries or stress
I really believe
Those times are the best

I refuse to become just like the rest
And foolishly run from impending death

Modern Circles

The new age family
Broken and lost
Torn between upbringings
Dad found another
Mom will get screwed
Well, financially
The time is wrong
Abstract confusion
Can I rise above this unfortunate setback?
No monetary reason I can't!

For Betterment

Benign and free
To work I won't go
There is much better for me

Cherubic faces and sordid thoughts
Explicit pleasures not found
I keep trying but my engine is stalled
Several doubts now abound

The sun shines brightly to console the floor
Who has a most mundane existence
We keep attempting to better ourselves
But fail for lack of persistence

First Encounter

Susceptible eyes view the confusion
Forced to make a connection
Concocting truths, to be only his
Wait 'til his first affections
Things turn around and a new day erupts
Several epiphanies he incurs
Feelings of anger, placidity and lust
He prays his motives aren't deferred

Contours

Beautiful human, so soft and so smooth
Hop in the car for a hypnotic cruise
Look at your contours, those wanton eyes
Do as you please but just tell me more lies

Where were you from, what was your name
I tell you the truth, I'm all but inane
Poet in disguise—this cloak's the best
Aspiring original unlike the rest

I need your assistance to cajole my thoughts
The children in my mind, with fear they are wrought
Nowhere to go with all these aimless games
A nobody's hero, where is my fame?

Epistle to Captain Clark

(In memory of the bravery and dedication of the men of the Corps of Discovery)

Oh, will you travel with me to the lands that lay far
Oh, will you come with me, my friend William Clark
Times will be difficult and you will often want home
But we were meant to discover, we were meant to roam

I can't imagine the very strange things we will see
The outstretched wilderness where all may roam free
Are you up for a journey, lacking stasis and rest
Are up for an adventure through the vast lands out West

It is a journey not finished by the great James Mackay
Him an Evans came home before finding a way
We'll travel the rivers which are so great and so wide
When times are the hardest in you I'll confide

////Reply////

My dear friend Meriwether, I'll meet up with you shortly
I can use the exercise as it seems I've grown portly
I'll bring my slave York, he has quite the back
To portage when necessary and bring up the slack

Yes, shortly I'll come and we can develop a plan
To reach the Pacific, I know that we can
Thanks for the offer; this will be quite the endeavor
We'll be etched in history and remembered forever

Why

Confounding relationships is my pet peeve
My feelings ignored, superfluous and light
Why am I always disassembled in the end?
Getting good at experiencing the knives of strife

Soft Spoken Angel

Soft spoken angel, the material of myths
Dichotomy to one, explore my pith
Angels of Mercy have blessed me with you
The present seems perfect as my hopes ensue

In the past, I have not treated you right
I cannot blame you if you've lost your light
My latent love becomes emblazed when you're 'round
Just the thought of your loss keeps my head on the ground

Attention Diverted

The sun skips over the buildings
Apathetically basking the upper hillside
While the sidewalks tenaciously endure
The flapping of numerous feet upon it
People glancing blindly about
Completely unaware of the eyes
Judging and undressing them from above

Stalwart Love

When the bogs of depression close around me
And the truth is weighing in—
I think of my wife, my children and hopes
While praying our life together will never end.

I can make changes—a chance I do beg
For your love is certainly worth it
Please don't discard me for former mistakes
Have faith that we can work through this

Think of our children and their bright futures
Think of the great times we've had
Let's recapture the moments that created our love
And build a relationship that can forever last

The Violent Child

Loss of spiritualism?
Discipline disappearing?
Let's blame it on the devil—
He just keeps reappearing.

The answers seem elusive
No way to right the copious wrongs
I beg listen to your children
—please, help guide them along

Kids shooting kids
Let's sneak a gun into school
You shouldn't have picked on me
Just to make yourself look cool.

Now we are spinning in a spiral of violence
Our bestial drives we cannot silence
To turn it around, it's probably too late
Have we resigned the world to a fiery fate?

A Childish Influence

From the Iron Giant to Scooby, I soak it all in
These positive images my mind must defend
For in a few years they'll be gone and changed
Let's hope that the world does not mold them deranged
I wake to cartoons first thing in the morning
Brew my coffee and accept my internal mourning
At times they lack intelligence, wit and meaning
And sometimes appear quite dry and demeaning
Yet these memories with my children I will always treasure
For in a few years they'll encounter very difficult pressures
For now I must provide my unwavering guidance
And as many before me pay my cartooning penance

Ended Love

Memories and dreams from the past
Many of which were not destined to last
From our first love to alcohol abuse
And the little things that kept us amused

I must give up, there's something better out there
Create new memories and hopes to revere
With old friends gone and new ones not right
We can solemnly revel in each others plight

Our time is gone—the towels on the mat
Once I'm gone I'll never be back
Just understand, there's no time to be bitter
And know that I could never reconsider

In a world that seems to crush all that we try
To politicians who think that everyone's high
I know true dreams we can bring to bear
Change for the better in the absence of fear

Reciting the Past

The knife of lies shoved right in my heart
My adoration for life seeps away
I found I was her love by the night
She had another fool during the day

I read the signs but was to weak to act
For fear of losing yet another
I should have spoke my mind and been a man
Why do we even bother?

Conjugal ties—an ambiguous fate
To question whether it will last
Say or do just one wrong thing
And you'll end up crying o'er the past

Freedom of the Mind

Freedom of the mind and I like it
The laws haven't found me yet
I like the path I've discovered—
Like a band starting their first set

The freedom to write whatever I think
My respect to you dear Jack
New ideas festooned in my mind
It's time to start my attack

Convoluted beliefs, religions and hopes—
The end of perverted bliss is inevitable
Bombings, murders, babies in dumpsters
Some things not even conceivable

I might be ranting, but you know it's true
We've fondled the earth until she is through
The end of innocence, truth and ideals
To me this madness seems all to real

Memories of Grandfather Fading Away

Memories of my Grandfather ripped away and devoured by time,
I feel such shame for forgetting when in my mind I see my mother crying.
Memorial Day weekend is closing and his grave I did not visit,
Wrapped up in my frivolous follies, his memory my actions discredit.
I attempt to justify my actions by saying I'll visit his grave next year,
To pay homage to a man who as a child I held most dear.
Time seems so malicious and evil—a cancerous beast that I'm learning to rue,
Something to fear because with age my sanity I seem to lose.

The Earth's Closing

I look at the Earth rotting away
Waiting for that terrible day
When we see she has no more to spare
Then everyone will have a care.

Everything gone, we're dwindling away
Dead and gone, becoming the clay
We should have learned to leave her alone
Nothing now but scattered bones.

A Humorous End

Death, death, I do decree
Isn't the way to go
It isn't the thing for me
Don't you believe so?

What if I refuse to go
When my time card is punched
Is there anything I should know
Will God be out to lunch?

What will the afterlife reveal
Will I end up low
I don't think that I'll get fired
If I fail to show

The Breakup

Lonely.
World of confusion
No woman
Gone.
Disbanded relationship
Thought things were fine
Leave for the big city
Come back
It's ended.
Continue on—
Carrying myself with false happiness

How life has changed

The kids, the noise, the foot puncturing toys
Good Lord, what have I done?
Life was so fun at one time
The girls, the alcohol, the parties

Now it is nothing more than a shaken memory
As if I am reviewing the life of an unknown person
Now I must discard all remnants of impropriety
And be a loving husband and venerable father

I don't know if I can
I miss the fun, conviviality, and late night revelry
Can I return?
Not without sacrificing health and money.

I think I will try to make the change and stay here
I'll watch the kids fight the demons that I have battled
I'll try to arm them with the weapons
That will ensure their victory in an immoral world

False High

Coffee and chocolate
The false high
American way
Not enough time for health
Always on the move
Lack of sleep….
Need something for energy
A remedy for the fatigue
Has to be another way
Change of lifestyle?
Well, maybe later.

Unfounded Hate

Different colors
My tribe doesn't like your tribe
Hasty solution?
Let's kill each other
Destroy families, cultures, hope
Show our ignorance
Why should we try to work it out?
We're too used to fighting
We've never known another way
Time for change....

Seeking Direction

Skirting the boundaries of happiness
I can hear it, see it, taste it….
I can almost feel it
Wanting it, now!!
But, while reflecting on the corpus
Of my experiences
I'm not quite sure how I will attain it
Maybe I'll forage in one direction
One marginal step at a time
Yes, I will go from there

Desirous Poet

Desirous poet
Simply seeking recognition
Just a little attention over here
Not too much to ask, is it?
Published!!
Still means very little to me
Where's the reciprocation
For my "difficult to obtain" thoughts?

Life's a bust

When it is all over
When everything is done
When the time does come
That I will never again see the setting sun

When I'm laid to rest
To return to the dust
I'll most assuredly exclaim
"That certainly was a bust!"

Perfect World

Perfect little town
Perfect little church
Perfect parents
Me?
Evil.
Rejecting their values
That's right.
Their your values;
I'll design my own.

The Auld Days

Time to return
To the auld ways
The auld morals
Auld virtues
Why must our days be so difficult?
Many seem to have the answers
But few have the drive
To change things for the better
To return us to better ways
But the calling of the dollar
Changes what we crave

Heavenly Reservation

Call ahead now
To reserve a seat
In a place I understand
Is entirely hard to beat
Streets golden paved
No one will walk alone
But if that's not what you like
The alternative is brimstone
Mountains of fire
That can devour you alive
I think that I'll make my choice,
That place so heavenly high.

Times Forlorn

Lost times
Forgotten times
But not to dwell on the past
We continue to create times
To be lost and forgotten
In our future

Tenets

Sexual appetite
Ability to indulge in forbidden pleasures
Biblical tenets
Out of context?
Out of wedlock.
Yet I am willing and unwilling
Although able
I search for quality
Waiting for the right woman
To writhe in sin with

Lust

Liquid lust
Late night relief
I know her for what she truly is
Or for what I've become

It is time

There is no hope, the finale is near
The time for truth is very clear
Quit the lies, the truth in love
My help must come from far above

Absence of Shame

In the absence of shame
Comes inner freedom
No absolutes or constants
Turmoil—
With a grain of desire
Bereft of inhibitions
Happiness must follow

Cease and Desist

The compression in my skull, the problems keep mounting
My chances of success I keep discounting
A mind rife with ideas that flow free as a fountain
Yet my days of utter failure I strangely keep counting

Some day I will make it; success I will acquire
But the older I become, my outlook grows direr
Is there any means to escape from the deepening mire?
As my thoughts grow abject, my mind is for hire

Would anyone want it, do I have much to offer?
I don't want to sell out too cheap just to fill my coffers
Maybe it's the weather that creates this ominous mind-mist
I'll just order these dour thoughts to cease and desist!

Disappointment

Cliff notes for the soul
Do you trust?
Do you believe?
Numerous disappointments
Are catalysts for doubts
Conscious concerns
Sub-conscious destructive thoughts
Organized religion
An atrium of faith
Inherent to disappointment
I know they are only human
Is it selfish to expect better?

Fairy Tales

The delightfully soothing fairy tales of bygone days,
Enlighten our children's minds no more.
We've ambiguously glued them to inane cartoons,
While losing the lessons of time-honored lore.

Brave knights slaying dragons has lost its luster,
No falling sky or a worried Chicken Little,
Or a blithe Robin Hood robbing the rich for the poor,
Where's the breadcrumbs left by Hansel and Gretel?

The virtues espoused in these finely woven tales,
Remain very applicable in these tumultuous days,
Providing hope and reassurance where depression exists,
While helping to resolve some heartache and dismay.

Dust off those storybooks and pass on the magic,
That you experienced so many years ago,
And share with your children the priceless lessons,
That will help them develop characteristics of gold.

A Fatherly Husband's Worry

An idle mind ravaged with savage desire
An engaging moment will not arise
The focus has vanished; left to my instincts
Something to occupy and clarify I must devise

Fledgling hopes that quickly age and pass away
Where in hell do I go and how will I get there?
I can't forget my wife and kids; unwavering responsibilities
Disappointing them must be a husband and father's greatest fear

It can't be me

The depression has veiled my judgment
What are we truly worth?
I'm just here to pay taxes
And to later fill a cemetery plot
I've got to rid myself
Of this deplorable negativity
No vestige of happiness—
Can I find
Stop!!!!
Think….
It will destroy me
Please—give me a sign
Carnivorous hate, depart!!!
This isn't who I am
I'm a bright young man
Full of hope, education and future
Where's my epiphany
That will later bring me riches?
Greed.
It's not so bad, is it?
An international virus
Permeating every continent
But this can't be who I've become
Are these just unkempt vagaries
Or have I departed
From the Christian tenets
Instilled and spanked into me
So many forgotten years ago
I have completely burned myself
Charred and smoking
Composting down into bitter ashes
Now I must rise above it
Just as the mighty Phoenix
And present the changes
To my unsuspecting world

Leaves

The coarse wooden arms stretch towards the heavens
Creating black veins in the amber-dusk horizon
The crisp autumn breeze gently rustles the leaves
As they pine for the earth so enticing

The brittle leaves quickly transform with the motive
To depart before the harsh winter does arrive
Leaving their mighty bare-chested guardians
To awaken them when again they can thrive

Tempered Experience

Have you ever experienced the cold shake-off
Of a petty and vindictive heart
To rupture your soul and rip it down the seams
Will my mind ever again find the serene?

We slowly recover and once again begin the search
Thinking this time will be different, this time it will work
Yet once more my fragile levity is maliciously destroyed
I'll probably wind up spouting the abstractions of Freud

But I know the healing powers of time will repair once more
And I will return to the social scene to search and cavort
For each time I make the mistake of trusting another heart
My hope and respect for the human race will quickly depart

Winter's Arrival

Winter is languidly creeping into my life once more
With the brittle frail leaves it has settled its score
The landscape is changing from verdant to barren
The thrust of the cold is determined and daring

The history of seasons does permeate my mind
A reminder of the years which have been harsh and unkind
Soon will come snow, the relentless slick and the sleet
While my pleasant emotions buckle in chagrin and defeat

My energy has departed with the days of the heat
When we enjoyed family and friends while barbecuing meat
Now we huddle inside and plead for an end
Of this disastrous season when my mood does descend

The trees in their gaunt demeanor I deplore
Everything appears dismal of which I previously adored
The lush green days are now lying in state
To serve as a bitter reminder of our yearly fate

Viking Warriors

The prow of the ship breaks from the mist
Guided by the wicked face of plunder
Teeming with dozens of greedy Norsemen
Prepared to rip the village asunder

Terrified children flee for their lives
As their fathers are cut down in their prime
The women and children will be sold as slaves
A depressing end to their once peaceful times

The mighty Vikings move deeper inside
To rob from the monasteries
Are these people the devil's children?
The villagers do wonder grimly

After the Norsemen have taken all that they desire
They quickly retreat to their knorrs
To return to Scandinavia and proudly flaunt
Their numerous spoils of war

The Vikings' care not of the pain they've inflicted
And all of the lives they have brutally destroyed
But future encounters with these consummate warriors
Any survivors will be sure to avoid

The City

Symmetrical suburbs and confusingly twisted roadways
Conceal malicious political ties and lascivious gatherings
Cool and clean country air often times can't compete
With the indefatigable city and its effervescent beat
The country is nice, well…some of the time
But from the city emanates worldly realities
No cohesion exists behind false pretenses
Continual lies become the truths
Obedience to convoluted laws and ordinances
Can lead to a precarious perch at the bottom
With no sight of the top and gratifying peace
It is here the ideals of the past are forgotten

A Soldier Not Forsaken

A soldier eyes the heavens on a sand-swept Baghdad night
With thoughts of a glittering brown-eyed son to calm his mind
His thoughts begin a weary transition to the letters of loving support
Renewing a determination that can often be tough to find

He then considers previous soldiers that were so despised and hated
In spite of their determination, self-sacrifice and gallantry
From the Vietnam Veteran showered with hate and spit
To a heavenly soldier that willingly gave all upon Calvary

There is legion upon legion of those who have been forsaken
Yet this soldier is pleased to know that he is not one
For a loving wife and son armed with faith and a prayer
Will provide a protection against any earthly affront

With his head in his hands and the sound of mortars in the distance
He finds a soothing peace in a land filled with death
This soldier knows that the gift of faith he's been granted
Will sustain him long after he has drawn his final breath

The Search for Recollection

The meandering old roads still appear quite the same
As they did in my much earlier days
With a few new homes sprinkled about the hills
And more colorful signs to show us the way

I love returning to these memorable times
Recalling the people that I knew once before
Viewing the changes that I never expected
And the removal of antiquities that I once adored

As the years roll by I search more for my history
And little souvenirs to ensure my memories last
I feel obligated to seek out constant reminders
Of the people and places that comprised my life's cast

Scottish Castle

The castle grasps tightly to the crest of the hill
Like a stone giant rising above the gray mist
A determined mother protecting her children
From the wrath of England's crushing fist

Many a bonnie Scotsman she has seen slaughtered
Her walls stained with their blood and their tears
The wounded and dying gripping her cold stones
Begging for someone to relieve their fading fears

The heartless atrocities that her walls have witnessed
Would to most become regretfully numbing
But you can still feel the icy hand of death
In the great ruins that now stand here crumbling

Here I lay
Lizard's lair
Yesterday's today
Burned hope
Unroll a new path
For I will flourish

Dreams

Are you coming?
I'm going on a trip.
To where you ask?
Into my dreams.
You may learn something,
Like your unconscious isn't what it seems.

The Question of Confusion

I feel confused
About things unknown
What is going on
With this world of ours
Were Arthur and Jesus
Truly kings....
Mortal creatures
Until death—
Will our knowledge
Be fulfilled and realized
....or ended
But in the end
We know
Though greatly ignored
We will rot
Slowly, timidly
Feed the worms
It's all over
Death is approaching
You can't hide
Here it comes—
I'm tired.

Eternal Fairness

What if an atheist treats other well?
What if a Christian mistreats all?
Will the atheist go to Hell?
Are they as bad as the ones,
That in the sorrow of others dwell?

Call to Freedom

The brave Irish have for decades fought
For due respect and home rule
The English don't care for what they desire
They love for them to be their fools

Hidee-Hey, the bold nationalists
My how you've been treated unfairly
Beaten and killed throughout Belfast
And the sordid streets of Londonderry

Fighting for a cause that only few understand
And the world has tried to ignore
They take your rights and beat down your pride
And wonder why order can't be restored

You fight for your rights, tis' the only way
Because peaceful folks usually become slaves
The dispute may subside but will never end
For you are the mighty and the brave

Many have unfortunately resorted to alcohol
For it gives them a sense of pleasure and relaxation
It has helped to forget for a moment the suffering,
The battles, the losses and condemnation.

The Fruition of Destruction

This flippant, reeling and dizzying world
Has unwittingly shattered my mind
Writhing and changing without a wisp of remorse
To insanity I've been consigned

Nothing can ever remain simple or pure
The confusion continues to unfurl
No heroes remain to provide direction and hope
Please give us something with which we can cope

What became of all that was respectful and sacred
The memory of those cheerful times remains clear
Is there anyone who can deliver us a future once more
Free from the evils we've grown to abhor

Traditions of this nation being mutilated and slaughtered
The lines of hatred continue to grow much clearer
The years roll on as the world breaks apart
Are we realizing what the Romans once feared?

Disagreement

Here comes the migraine, never to part, as I think about the tangled web society has woven itself into. Everyone wants a fix; few attempt—but we really have no one to blame but everyone....attempt to fix it and you will be criticized.

No one will agree on a plan, too much disagreement and spite; that is our nature, really—to disagree
On abortion
On politics
On religion
On scoops of coffee...

Just add what you want to the list; no way out of it.

It could easily end in the destruction of all—
But....I'm sure there are those who would disagree with me on that.

9/11

The tears well up and won't go away
As I recall that terrible day
Thinking of how thousands lost their lives
The small children and their plaintive cries

The plumes of smoke consuming the streets
Cowardly terrorists touting our defeat
Families broken, never to be the same
An angry nation searching to blame

What can we do to help those that lost
Let's right this wrong no matter the cost
Well take them the fight, methodical and loud
And show them America is still standing proud

Hurry Mother Earth

The sun begins its orange-splashed plummet
From its fair cradle in the middle-sky
While the cooling winds from the harshening northwest
Remind us that cold times are nigh

The grumbling winter winds that make weary bones creak
To the cloud shrouded skies and the mental havoc it wreaks
I beg Mother Earth to quicken her run around our star
Is the yearly trip you must make really all that far?

Yet we will wait if we must for warmer times to arrive
For if your revolution would vary, I know we'd all die
So just take the time necessary to deliver spring once again
And I will do my best to remember what a good friend you have been

Temporal Morsel

The sharp sting of anxiety-ridden hopelessness
Skewers in the my chest
Can't be a heart attack, not at my age
Those things kill people at my fledgling point in life
Can't be…not that lucky.
I'm like the rest, so human, morally weak….and searching
I've quit searching for a healthy muse—
The bad ones are so much more fun!!
Yet they weaken and destroy both mind and body
Seared minds rife with confusing contempt
Becoming rage….
Accept age, weakness, and temporal existence
Good bye to the anxiety and worries
Possible?
Fun to preach but that is where it ends for me.
Maybe my coming age will marry wisdom, procreate, and give birth to happiness and satisfaction.
Although subjective, reaching it will be my own.
I'm sure one or many will be disappointed with the path I choose to wander.
…And wandering is what it should be called.

Solemn Approach

As Christmas begins its solemn and promised approach
It quickly marries up with the bills
Between the marketing of greed and the mounting expenses
I have somehow misplaced my youth-filled holiday thrill

It is difficult to feel thankful when we constantly must worry
About our finances, employment and future
Yet I don't want to say "farewell" to the seasonal tidings of joy
And risk compromising my children and their untainted nature

Their fresh little eyes still believe in the goodness of man
And gregariousness of the renowned Santa Claus
But the moral focus that parents must fight to maintain
Seems to teeter between failure and fall

Although these principles we battle to instill
Appear to rest upon a foundation of sand
Love, persistence and our unwavering guidance
Well lead them away from a life of perpetual reprimand

Thunderstorm

The mild grumbling moving in from the west
Swells quickly into a roar
Spotted shadows paint the grass
And the rain begins to pour

The raging howls of the wind and the rain
Carry on for a half-hour or more
Giving way to the breaking skies
Which will bestow upon us sunlight once more

Pulling Away

I am pulling away,
I have no desire to follow,
Your blind and shifty fundamentalism,
Which equates to a discriminatory prison.

Please take your leave,
You disgraceful hypocrite,
You put others down so easily,
Depart before your evil permeates me.

Your belief is a cult,
No better than many,
Why not try using your gifted mind,
Never know what you may find.

Omnipotence

The terrible weight of omnipotence
Knowing all….
Seeing all….
Hearing all….
Feeling all….
The yearning to get involved…
….I like being a limited mortal

The Shadows

The shadows do wistfully beckon,
Welcome to the wily world of my dreams,
Let us first confront your latent fears,
I promise you, there is no hidden scheme.

Druid law.
Earth justice.
Every living creature was created with reason.
Do not make the mistake of fearing the unknown.
Head first into the rewarding world of inner truth.

Ubiquitous Youth

Cold dissecting stares
"A new face!" their brains cry.
How to confront the awkward moment
The face displays the disdainful lies

Stark and acrid fear conceived
You cannot run from us
The young are truly bright stars
With anger filled eyes of lust

Everyone knows how you truly feel
There is no point in trying to deceive
Don't smother us with your feigned concerns
From me you'll get no reprieve

The Quiet Torture of Marriage and Child Rearing

Mixed messages in a perplexing marriage
The knot tied around my neck
Mixed messages whilst raising kids
Some form of sanity I do beck

It doesn't seem to matter at the moment
Maybe in the end it will all work out
Then again I might experience a messy divorce
…then celibacy I will tout

Damn these extremely stressful commitments
Former centuries have made protocol
It's been imbued in the annals of time
What in the end will become of us all

I need to find something to placate my mind
Before the stresses do suck me under
Be gone with the headaches, misfortunes and confusion
No longer will my mind bounce asunder

Success in short

Love, the yeast of life
Living in an unleavened hell
Success in short….
Stay single

Shackled

I'm growing tired of the pain, the hurt and despair
My hopes strewn about leaving me exposed and bare
I can't live without her, but with her I'm bitter
Dubious desires causing my demons to titter

There must be an out, escape is paramount
Death won't work; the pain continues to surmount
Sex is the pivot that might help me think straight
Even if she isn't the one, clearly not my soul mate

Then why can't I bolt, this country is free
Yet wherever I go, will my conscious shackle me?
I do still love her; the pain is who I am
But with it I am forced to live amongst the damned

Redirection

The joy of Christmas in a young child's eyes
Can bring levity to guilt stricken heart
Praying that their innocence and love is not lost
While providing for us a fresh start

Life and lost love can quickly break our spirits
Creating a world of cynicism, greed and despair
Sending the once blissful into a spiral of self-destruction
From where often no escape will appear

The bulk of our hardships we carry in our minds
If somehow we could just learn to let go
Of what we believe to be wrongs and inequities
Why can't we view the world as we did long ago?

Many have heard the chortle of several demons
As they argue that the negative thoughts are just fine
Yet remember you must not fall for these beguiling lies
If you are to avoid the cancerous poisoning of your mind

Rapturous Turmoil

Fresh, young hope
I love new female prospects
Always sad timing
Oooh, what rapturous turmoil
Choking me with a serpents coil
A most resplendent gathering
Of loving social destruction

Memory of a song

The torrent of memories triggered by a song
Can be most haunting and profound
From a funeral of a friend to a homecoming dance
Sweet melodies can take us back home

Some memories we'll embrace and others deplore
But they will hang with us nonetheless
For the melodies have become the memories
From which the radio can always bring us back

The collection of notes that we call a song
Can deliver us unto much better times
But we must live our lives as it is given
And find new songs and memories to enshrine

Life Misunderstood

I've encountered piercing difficulties
Understanding the malleable rules of my life
I've tried so hard to do what thought was right
But it's created nothing but a life rife with strife

It seems the more money I acquire
The more expenses I seem to find—
Nickel and dime me to an untimely death
Will I reach retirement before I pull my final breath?

What is my drive, that thing that keeps me going?
My family, my wife, the fact that I'm free?
I need a plan, or an outline for my future
Where in world am I going and what should I be?

Inner child then and now

Younger faces and visions from the past
Remind me of those good-ol-days
When times at school seemed so tough and intolerable
Social life seemed to permeate our ways

What I would give to return to those days
Knowing then what I think I now know
My grades would soar and life I would enjoy
Much deeper friendships I would work to sow

Now it's taxes, kids, lack of money and work
That seems to make our days feel so cruel
Responsibilities have a way of squelching our fun
We now play the parent as opposed to the fool

Yet I must learn to accept these significant changes
While recalling all of the places I've been
And live my life for my children
While vicariously existing through them

Amorousness

Copious doubts
A flood of mindless thoughts
The need to enhance myself
Into the quagmire I delve
For her....
Affection with such fervor
I want to live blissfully....
Happily sappy
Devotion.
Today and everyday
Accept what I say
I have paved the way
To a future so strong
Not to be proved wrong
This feeling prolonged
Infectious is my song
With this I'll move on...

Happiness and Satisfaction

Think about what in your life you've done
To make this revolving rock a place any better
Yeah, you're working to pay taxes and buy this and that
But do these things ever really matter

What have you accomplished in your brief time
That has truly brought you lasting happiness
Possessions on Earth will not provide lasting satisfaction
Unless family and friends are the source of your bliss

Printed in the United States
71192LV00004B/269